be

Embracing Attitudes for a Strong Healthy Marriage

Marc *and* Mildred Clark

Unless otherwise noted, Scripture quotations are taken from the Holy Bible, New International Version®, NIV®. Copyright © 1973, 1978, 1984, 2011 by Biblica, Inc.™ Used by permission of Zondervan.

Cover models: Angel Ceara Clark & Dashawn Peterson
Cover photography by David Grinage
Cover design by Loren D. Clark

Urithi Nyumba
Memphis, TN 38119

ISBN: 978-0-578-62243-9

Library of Congress Control Number: 2020902584

Commendations

My wife Casey and I have watched and learned from the Clarks example many times in our marriage. I am excited for others to share in their wisdom as we have. This book is a much needed resource in this day and age." Their love for each other, their family—immediate and chosen—and for Christ and others is so evident and contagious.

—Caleb Sigler, Elder/Pastor of Worship Mosaic Church Memphis

"The authors' attention to detail, their passion, and the love they have for couples can be felt throughout this book. The desire for couples to succeed comes through on every page. Also, putting your life's experiences into a book is not always easy. However, they pulled this off in grand fashion.

—Danny and Amelia Cole, Executive Pastor & Elder of New Growth in Christ Christian Center • Founders of Aquila & Priscilla Marriage Ministries

Marc and Mildred are sharing principles that are tried and proven in their own marriage. Those who apply these principles are people who have purposely planned to be fruitful and have longevity in their love relationship. As a social worker, it is my opinion that this book is much needed in building strong families within this current generation.

—*Wendy Barringer, Social Worker, TN Dept. of Children's Services*

"This book is a wonderful tool that can help even the best of marriages become better. It's a great resource for newly married couples, people who have been married before, and couples who have been married for years. I love that it touches both the natural and spiritual aspects of marriage-togetherness. And, it offers time to reflect, realize, and readjust certain aspects of who we truly are, in order to be.

—*Deborah E. Harris, DNP*

Dedications

In Loving Memory of Our Parents:
Bishop Loyce F. Clark
Estella Clark
Catherine "The Great" Miller

For Our Children:
Terence

Loren

Angel

Kim

Dustin & Rachel

Sherman & Precious

Nikia

Kenneth

For:
Every individual, couple, and family we have been
afforded opportunity to serve.

Acknowledgements

*T*he creation of this written work exists because of the concerted effort of a great many people. We are forever grateful!

We are grateful to the individuals, couples, and families who we have been graced to serve. We appreciate each of you who willingly shared your feelings, opinions, disappointments, setbacks, and successes regarding your life and relationships. We are honored and humbled that you have been part of our journey.

Family and friends—Social Media connections included—who have prayed for, inspired, encouraged, and pushed us to sit down and get the job done. Special shout-out to Eddie Miller, Carolyn Miller, Wendy Barringer, Tiffany Marshall, Brenda Green, and Domeniek Harris.

Writer and Literary Coach, Sharai Robbin, for coaching us through our writing process and thoroughly editing and adding luster to our finished manuscript.

Contents

Preface

ow!!!! This book has been a journey—an important part of our (Marc and Mildred's) venture to help others avoid much, if not all, the twists, turns, and roller coaster rides we endured on this journey to oneness in marriage. We were married at the tender age of 19 —freshmen in the art of marriage. Though we considered ourselves mature for our ages, we were unaware of the challenges that existed on the other side of "I DO." Like many couples, we had slanted views—two perspectives (his and hers) intertwined with our familial beliefs—Marc coming from a nuclear family and Mildred from a one-parent household—as to what marriage was and what it should look like. We were both believers and were active members in our local church. However, neither leadership nor married couples among this body of people would openly and honestly discuss the issues and challenges of marriage.

The writ of the Word, such as "Husbands love your wives as Christ loved the church and gave himself for it," and "Wives submit yourselves to your own husbands," were often quoted and used as a source of keeping marriages whole; however, little to no practical tools were offered. There were no truly defining moments of what submission really looked like and no clarifying messages to the men regarding the full measure of the Christ kind of love. When it was asserted that men should love their wives as Christ loved the church, there was no follow through on what this type of love encompassed. What we often witnessed was one sided. The wives, more often than not, had to bear the brunt of any problems that arose in their relationships. Almost every state of conflict was attributed to the woman not being submissive enough. This led to tremendous discord.

As we faced our trials—clashing like Titans—we realized that if our relationship would stand a chance of enduring, we had to do something. So, since our church did not have what we needed in this area, we searched for workshops, seminars, and conferences where we could learn, develop, and utilize the tools needed to walk together as one. We also sought to connect with wise couples who were successfully doing life together. We wanted to glean from their wisdom and knowledge in order to avoid unnecessary stumbling blocks. We intentionally set out to do the work necessary to have a strong, healthy, sustainable, and great union. We attended every marriage conference and retreat we could and shed many tears as we travailed and pushed through communication, decision making, and daily family problems that made every other situation look gigantic.

It was during our personal journey that we were ignited with a flame of passion to be part of the solution in salvaging all facets of relationships and saving marriages–especially among those in the household of faith.

With the blessings of our father and Bishop (The Honorable Loyce F. Clark), who has transitioned from this life, we are walking in our purpose as the Spirit of God leads. Not only do we have a desire to teach what we have acquired through experience and study, we want to be an example and a living testimony to everyone the Father assigns our paths to cross. We want the world to know that relationships, especially marriages, can and do stand the test of time. When we are willing to do the work and adjust our unrealistic expectations, behaviors, and attitudes, doing life together becomes a true walk of love and grace. In *be: Embracing Attitudes for a Strong, Healthy Marriage*, you will find the gentle and guided instruction that we ourselves longed for. These are things we discovered that are not set on automatic just because two people exchange nuptials. These things require knowing, premeditation, and willful intentionality.

Unlike a daily devotional, and because life deals a different hand at different stages of life, there is no direct order in which the *be* attitudes contained in this text have to be read or utilized. This book is your resource. You are free to choose where you need and want to begin, and you can revisit the pages as often as needed or desired.

It is our hope and prayer that this printed work will serve as a motivational tool and resource to assist you with being intentional in monitoring and adjusting specific behaviors and attitudes that are subject to hindering your relationship success. Instead of creating hostility in your marriage and other relationships, you can change the atmosphere and experience a strong, healthy, enduring marriage—a marriage that can stand the test of time. So, let's get started on our journey of being and becoming our best selves, by embracing and developing the right attitudes.

Introduction

*T*here is no human experience more sacred, more beautiful, or more joyous than two people standing before God, family, and friends smiling, and vowing to love each other through the best and worst of times. But, despite coming together in matrimony and making a solemn promise "to love and cherish each other for better and for worse, in sickness and in health, for richer or poorer, forsaking all others until death do us part, a number of marriages do not survive. Why? The answers are numerous and varied—communication, infidelity, sexual problems, destructive patterns, values and beliefs, life stages, stress, trauma, jealousy, and even boredom can attribute to failed marriages.

The year 2019 marked 25 years that we, Marc and Mildred Clark, have served our community as ambassadors promoting and educating others on what it takes to create, build and sustain strong, healthy relationships. Although we focus much on marriage and family, we believe the skills needed for success in marriage and family life are developed throughout our existence.

> *Take time to prepare before the pomp and circumstance.*

For us, having a strong, healthy, and sustainable marriage is as much about preparation as it is about preservation.

Over and over again, we meet people who spend much of their time, energy, and resources planning for a spectacular wedding with little to no regard or preparation time for actually being married and becoming husband and wife. The lack of attention and awareness to the importance of preparation before the pomp and circumstance often leads to problems when two people actually have to live and do life together.

Because many choose not to, or are unaware that premarital support through coaching, mentoring, and/or counseling can potentially have a significant positive effect on their relationship, they have qualms about sharing and receiving information. Others are hesitant to seek guidance because they have witnessed more unstable than stable marriage relationships. Their confidence is flawed when it comes to seeking out wise counsel. Many

> *Each of us need help navigating through challenges.*

think their marriage will be different; they do not consider that they too will be faced with a level of challenges that can rock the very core of their union.

"'Kain't' nobody tell me nothing about what I need to do for my husband/wife," is a statement we have heard thousands of times in various settings where relationship counseling and coaching have entered the conversation. The truth is, people need help navigating through the challenges of relationship building just as we did, but often will neither seek nor accept it. So, when that thin line between love and hate or indifference is reached, a couple is at a crossroad and begins questioning, "Will I stay or will I leave?" Unfortunately, it is often the latter, resulting in joining the statistical rank and category of failed marriages.

Marriages tend to fall into one of three categories—good, tolerable, and failure. Although failure is only one-third of these classifications, it remains tragic and heart-wrenching when marriages reach this point. Except for a few, if any, no one stands and commits to exchanging marital vows with the intention of abandoning or being abandoned by their spouse. Yet, sometimes divorce is placed on the table, and it happens. Nonetheless, we are aware and have witnessed that marriages can be resuscitated from a point of despair. When a couple makes the decision to put sincere effort towards doing the work as prescribed in this text, they can experience the peace and joy of creating, building, and sustaining a strong, healthy, loving, and enduring bond.

This book is created to encourage people to think about marriage improvement and to cultivate marriage transformation. In this text, we will take a look at 25 specifically selected *be* attitudes that we pray you will add to your weapons of warfare to protect your union. Why 25? We chose 25 because the number denotes wisdom, favor, goodwill, generosity, kindness, and indulgence; it signifies the interminable giving of grace upon grace.

In regard to relationships, the number 25 represents the beginning of more exciting milestones and the importance of being adaptable and versatile in our unions. This number represents important transformations, which encompass growth and the power to perpetually be and

> *Change is inevitable.*

become the couples we are destined to be in and out of change.

In marriage, as in life, change is inevitable. With this in mind, you need to be strong, courageous, and wise. When the going gets tough, we encourage married couples to hold on to the faith that everything will work out for the good of you and your spouse. Taking the journey and bringing into effective action the tools presented here will assist you in living an abundant life and having a more meaningful existence together.

The information compiled in this writing is constructed to guide couples who desire to enrich, elevate, and enhance their marital relationship. We share these *be* attitudes, which if implemented and practiced, will move marriages from dreadful, good, weak, despairing, inferior, antagonizing, and half-hearted situationships, to pleasant, great, strong, joyful, superior, gratifying, and fully-committed relationships. We have both witnessed and are testaments that strong, healthy marriages can be created, built, and sustained when two people willingly and intentionally do the work. Let us begin our journey not only of living and moving, but our journey to be.

1

Be Accountable

"Wisdom lies in our willingness to be accountable."
Mildred Clark

One of the most overlooked dynamics in the process of creating

Accountability is one's willingness to accept responsibility for his actions.

and experiencing a successful marriage is accountability. Accountability is one's willingness to accept responsibility or to account for his/her actions. This is important in all aspects of life and in every relationship, which includes marriage, family, friendship, and work. Accountability includes surrounding yourself with others who speak life and wisdom into you and your marriage. Being accountable invites others to help us with our weaknesses, and it is an essential part of building a great marriage. We must understand that we are not created to do life alone.

> *The purpose for the practice of accountability is to create an atmosphere that breeds security and reliability.*

For, "No Man is an Island." This is especially true in marriage. Therefore, it is important that a couple chooses to be accountable one to the other. This means that no major decisions should be made without consulting your spouse. The purpose for the practice of accountability is to create an atmosphere that breeds security and reliability. This way of living is when two people walk together as a united "we" instead of just "me." With this in mind, it is necessary that a couple finds the perfect balance between the two because "me" should never win over "we."

It is also imperative that individuals and couples have people in their lives who are filled with wisdom and insight, who will serve as accountability agents or partners—those willing to love you for real, without enabling you to continue to make unwise choices. Your spouse can also be such an agent, but each of

Connect with seasoned individual and couples who are walking in wisdom.

us must be willing to submit to wisdom regardless of where and from whom it comes.

It's wise to connect with seasoned individuals and couples who are willing to walk with you through your journey to oneness in marriage and in unity with others.

Let's Do It!

Make sure you consult with one another about important decisions. Make it a continual and normal practice. DO NOT make any critical decisions without your spouse's input. In addition, seek out and connect with wise individuals—friends and seasoned individuals who will help you be and become better by telling you the truth, in love. Be open and willing to embrace the truth and make the necessary adjustments to improve.

2

Be Affectionate

"We can live without religion and meditation, but we cannot survive without human affection."

Dalai Lama

Oftentimes, we have been led to believe that love is a feeling. However, it is our belief that love is

> Affection serves as the super highway between our heads and our hearts.

greater than a feeling. It is a verb; it is action, and we make the choice to put love in motion through affection. Affection is ACTIVE LOVE. It

> *The very essence of our being is wired for touch.*

is affection that serves as the super highway between our heads and our hearts. This act of love is experienced not only through affectionate words being whispered in the ear, but through the sense of touch—the first of the five senses each of us develops.

The very essence of our being is wired for touch. When words are not enough, the need for positive touch and the reassurance and the connection it produces is unfathomable. This non-verbal communication encompasses tenderness, compassion, love, gratitude, happiness, and safety. It is undoubtedly one of our most fundamental needs and is the secret weapon in a number of successful relationships.

Touch remains as essential for adults as it does for babies. A positive touch can change the atmosphere and cause one to smile, relax, breathe, and feel secure.

One such touch of affection is the hug. Research reveals that each of us needs a daily dose of hugs. How many hugs a day are sufficient? Well, the choice is yours and is based on your needs for survival, maintenance, and growth. It is said that we need hugs four times a day for survival, eight times a day for maintenance, and twelve times a day for growth. The point is that hugging is universally comforting, and the benefits go beyond the warm feeling.

> *Hugging lowers cortisol and increases oxytocin.*

Not only does a hug feel good, it releases healing and yields positive side effects. Hugging lowers cortisol levels—the hormone responsible for stress, high blood pressure, and heart disease. Hugging increases levels of oxytocin—the love hormone that serves to intensify a couple's bond. When touch is positive and oxytocin is released, it has the power to solidify your relationship, ease stress, induce sleep, foster generosity, and boost sexual arousal. In addition, the proper hug crystallizes our emotional memories. It helps our minds to store and remember information clearly.

> *Distribute healing through the power of touch to your spouse, children, and others.*

We believe positive physical touch, which includes hugging, is one of the gifts of healing, and we want to challenge you to distribute healing through the power of touch to your spouse, children, and others who are receptive and with whom you feel comfortable.

Let's Do It!

Give your spouse a 20-second hug minimum before you go your separate ways and when you come back together. It's a great way to send each other off in the morning and to greet each other in the afternoon. As a matter of fact, when it is possible, do it throughout the day just because it feels good to embrace and be embraced. Then, expect great benefits.

3

Be Affirming

"As random raindrops can help calm a rough sea, so can a kind word smooth a furrowed brow. Yes, the words that come out of your mouth matter."

Mildred & Marc Clark

An important truth we should never render invalid is that like each of us, the people in our lives stand

> The words
> we speak
> matter.

in need of emotional support. If married, this is especially true of our spouses. We must remember that the words we speak matter, and keep in mind the importance of speaking life-giving, heartfelt words that serve as beacons of inspiration, enthusiasm, and encouragement—conveying honor, value, and importance.

It is imperative that we understand the power we wield when we open our mouths to speak. The words we allow to proceed from our lips have the potential to release into the atmosphere either negative or positive vibes. Our words have the power to tear down or build up. We should, therefore, choose to lean toward the positive. Our desire should be to speak life and declare blessings into the hearts and minds of those we love.

Affirmations should be genuinely expressed.

Affirmations should be genuinely expressed because we see another's gifting, recognize who they are, what they bring to the table, and intentionally highlight those things. Our words should be like the sounds of soft, calming music, and fall upon the ears of the listener like the soft landing of a butterfly. We need to avoid letting even one rotten word seep out of our mouths. Instead, we should offer only fresh words that build others up when they need it most. This way our good words will communicate grace to those who hear them. (Eph. 4:29, The VOICE).

> Let your words be another's muse.

So, as you go forth living, moving, and being, let your words become another's muse, causing them to meditate on the fact that they are important and their presence is needed in the world and in your life.

Let's Do It!

Give affirmation! It is needed, desired, and necessary. Tell your spouse how important s/he is. Highlight the good qualities they possess. (e.g. "I love waking up beside you in the morning." "I feel safe with you.") Make life-giving affirmations an everyday intentional practice until it becomes a daily way of moving in and through the world.

4

Be Agreeable

"Hav the anointed one been split up into many pieces? ...
Absolutely NOT"
1 Corinthians 1:13, The VOICE

Many have a tendency to operate in relationships in the mode of disagreement. "Let's agree to disagree!" is often the assertion of the day. However, when

Agree
to
agree.

this statement is made, disagreement is frequently left unresolved, resulting in contention instead of accord. Because of this, we would like to challenge this method of thinking and encourage you—especially in relationship matters—to change the mantra to, "Let's agree to agree."

We do understand that two people will not always have the same viewpoint. Nonetheless, we believe couples can walk in agreement without having the same opinion. Being in agreement does not require us to copy and paste someone else's perspective. It does require compromise where each side makes agreeable concessions—not grudgingly or hesitantly, but from a position of power.

> In marriage, the intent is to walk and serve together as one.

Like Paul asserted to the Church at Corinth, we want to encourage couples and families to "...come together in agreement not allowing anything or anyone to create division [between]/among you... Be restored, completely fastened together with one mind and shared judgement...[not] consumed by fighting and petty disagreements" (I Corinthians 1:10, The Voice). Moreover, in the old testament, Amos asked the question, "Can two people walk together without agreeing on the direction" (Amos 3:3, NLT)? The answer is clearly, "No."

In marriage the intent is to walk and serve together as one, but it cannot be done effectively if we choose disagreement over agreement. Experience has

> *We wanted the music of our lives...to be a pleasing arrangement of parts.*

left us no doubt that agreeing to disagree is easy. Spouses as well as other individuals can diverge to neutral corners—as Marc and I did on many occasions—and choose to never address the problem. This produces a spirit of disharmony. When we understood that agreement takes work, we decided that we would no longer walk together with dissonance. We wanted the music of our lives, as we journeyed together, to be a pleasing arrangement of parts—congruous instead of a cacophony of harsh inharmonious sounds— even in the loudness of silence.

Let's Do It!

Based on the order of importance, prioritize your input regarding your viewpoint on a particular topic or issue. Before you speak, ask yourself, 1) Is what I have to say true, necessary, and kind? 2) Will it make things better and bring harmony to the situation? 3) Will it be understood? 4) Is it the right time to speak?

5

Be Attentive

"Those who are self-effacing and attentive become the recipients of confidences."
-Thornton Wilder

*H*ave you stopped paying attention to your marriage, family, and other important relationships? If so, it is time to shift. It is time to have a sense of "with-it-ness." In other words, be relentless in your awareness of what is and/or is not going on in your relationships—especially with your spouse.

In a world where technology abounds and life is fleeting, our attention is pulled, yanked, and split into a plethora of directions—work, errands, computer blogs, social media, mobile phones, tablets—in addition to maintaining strong, healthy relations with our spouses, friends, and family.

> *Your spouse is your first priority...Be your spouse's biggest fan, supporter, comforter, and confidant.*

Throughout this written work, you will note that we are advocates of intentionality, and when it comes to attentiveness, it is vital.

Relationships with friends and extended family are valuable and need attention. If you are married, however, your spouse is your first priority. You must remember that nothing and no one is more important than your mate. In good and bad times, be your spouse's biggest fan, supporter, comforter, and confidant. Keep your love alive by giving it the nourishment needed to perpetually grow and develop into a strong, healthy, and enduring relationship. Be thoughtful and considerate of your spouse's needs; think about him and be present. Pay careful attention to the things that bring out the best in him as well as the things that cause travail.

> *Pay careful attention.*

Let's Do It!

Show your attentiveness in your relationships —in marriage by writing your spouse love notes, doing things your spouse wants to do, going out on a date, and if applicable, ministering together. In marriage and extended relationships, listen to hear. Ask questions and make a note of what's going on in their lives. Send affirmations and "thinking about you" text messages. Be a good friend on and off social media. Do more together, and most importantly, when you are together, "GET OFF THE PHONE." Put the mobile phone down and back away. Last, but not least, be a person of your word, do what you say you're going to do; otherwise, do not make promises you cannot keep.

6

Be Committed

"Let us be honest... The threat to marriage... is a lack of loving commitment—whether it is found in the form of neglect, indifference, cruelty, or adultery, to name a few manifestations of the loveless desert in which too many marriages come to grief."

-Malcolm Turnball

*C*ommitment is more than a declaration; it is an action-oriented undertaking. It is not a 50/50 exchange. It requires two individuals ready to commit 100% to the relationship and choosing to love, honor, and cherish each other through life—the good, better, and best of it as well as in the days of trouble. It is the willingness to make sacrifices for the needs and best interest of the one you vowed to love, honor, and cherish. Commitment includes doing the work that focuses on monitoring and adjusting personal perspectives instead of making attempts to change your partner.

> If we're not fully committed to making our relationships work, they won't work.

A study analysis of 172 married couples conducted by UCLA psychologists confirms that commitment is not what we do when things are going well; it is what we do when faced with challenges. It is having determination, making sacrifices, and taking active steps to sustain a strong, healthy relationship.

> *Commit to the commitment.*

It is important in any relationship, but especially marriage, that we perpetually choose to commit to the commitment that we make one to the other. Otherwise, it doesn't matter how much counseling or coaching we get, how much advice or how many books we read. If we're not fully committed to making the relationship work, it won't work.

Let's Do It!

Revisit the vows you made on your wedding day. Reflect on and keep the promises you made to your spouse. Serve your spouse in LOVE and sprinkle it with grace.

Marc & Mildred Clark

7

Be Covered

"Like a bird protecting its young, God will cover you with His feathers, will protect you under His great wings; His faithfulness will form a shield around you, a rock-solid wall to protect you."

Psalm 91:4, VOICE

It is important on this journey called life that we understand we are not

We are not meant to do life alone.

meant to do life alone—separate from our Creator, the Eternal One. Neither do we have to do marriage alone. What does this mean? It means because we are made in the image and likeness of our Creator King, He desires to walk with us in our daily lives. Because He is our Creator, He knows exactly how we are to function in and through life. It is, therefore, wise to remain under God's covering, which allows Him to be the overseer of our lives—including our marital union.

> *Allow God to be the equalizer, the balancer that keeps you centered and in tune with what is good and right in serving each other.*

By submitting ourselves and our relationship to God, we allow Him to be our equalizer, the balancer that keeps each of us centered and in tune with what is good and right in serving each other.

When we allow the Eternal One to take the lead, our relationships become a reflection of Christ's interconnection with the church—the universal body of Christ. For it is the Children of the Kingdom—not the institutional structures we attend—that the Eternal One is both within and in fellowship and relationship with. This is also the only efficient and effective way for a man to cover his wife. The husband himself must be adequately covered under the headship/leadership of One greater than himself—the Creator King.

When a couple, a two-strand cord, allows God to become a ligature among them, the two strands become three, and the union becomes stronger and tighter, and is not easily separated into

We need both spiritual and practical principles that are reliable and sound.

pieces as a result of a blow, shock, or strain.

In life's journey, when we agree to accept the mission of matrimony and declare this acceptance before the Eternal One, we are invoking His spiritual influence into our relationship. In order for the mission to be successful, we need to include the spiritual application of order as well as practical principles.

Let's Do It!

Consider this. Neither your life nor your marriage journey has to be experienced alone. Connect with the Creator King and allow him to have rulership, not only in your life, but in your relationship with your spouse. Pray daily for each other and speak life and love into the atmosphere. Invite the Spirit of God to rest, rule, and abide in each and every nook and cranny of your union. Where He leads, follow. Run to Him—not from him—in challenging times, so you will always be covered under His umbrella of wisdom, safety, and protection.

Be Determined

"There is no chance, no destiny, no fate, that can circumvent, hinder, or control the firm resolve of a determined soul."
Ella Wheeler Wilcox

*D*etermination is the twin of commitment. It is one's ability to stand firm in purpose and resolution. It is moving progressively in a fixed direction towards a goal no matter

> A couple's greatest task is to develop strength of character.

what challenges are faced. This unwavering persistence is often seen in pursuing a career or obtaining a college degree. This same or greater level of focus and direction is essential in marriage.

The greatest task in marriage is to develop the strength of character and intentionality that results in a lifelong relationship—an alliance and partnership that will stand the test of time. Once two people have made a commitment to each other, they must consciously determine within themselves and with each other that regardless of the obstacles, they will make it.

Based on the legally established grounds for divorce, this determination does not include abuse, adultery, and abandonment. On the other hand, there are instances where infidelity did not strangle the marriage. Couples that make the choice to work through infidelity decide to

> *Do the required work necessary to produce healing in your relationship.*

do the required and often extensive work to produce the healing necessary to move forward in the relationship. Although it takes work, Marc and I have met with and ministered to couples whose determination and sincere repentance gave them the strength needed to continue thriving together on their journey.

Let's Do It!

Oftentimes, we show tremendous determination when it comes to achieving things we are passionate about in life (e.g.

education, successful careers). This will-power does not give in to the fear of failure, and things will inevitably be crossed off our list. Examine those areas in your life where you are most determined. Then, develop this same level of willpower and single-mindedness when it comes to your union. Be more obstinate in creating an atmosphere for the success of your life together.

9

Be Divorce Proof

"If every man would make his prime concern the comfort and well-being of his wife and every wife makes her chief concern the comfort and well-being of her husband, we would have very little divorce in the land."

Gordon B. Hinckley

ew couples, if any, get married to get divorced; yet, divorce continues to happen at an alarming rate. According to the American Psychological Association, out of the 90% of people who get married by age 50, 40-50% get divorced; and the divorce rate for those who remarry is even higher.

Oftentimes, when individuals remarry, they do so without having learned to work out relational issues. Getting remarried is not the cure. Those who do not learn to work out issues in their first marriage will likely carry over their same code of conduct, habits, or preferences into the next relationship, ultimately leading to another divorce. It is to this end that we fervently remind couples that in order for marriage to work, you have to do the work to make it work, and end the cycle of divorce.

> *In order for marriage to work, you have to do the work to make it work.*

So, how does a couple divorce-proof their marriage? One of the best ways is preparation before marriage. Do not negate really getting to know the one you plan to do and spend life with. Get to know the family; ask questions. Make sure the person you're interested in has no problem having hard conversations. There are seven things we recommend individuals discuss with a potential lifelong companion. These seven things are: Family (all aspects), Religion, Finance, Food, Politics, Sex, and Social Life. As the Honorable Judge Mablean Ephriam would say, "Look deep before you leap." Therefore, during this process of discovery, pay attention to any red flags that show up,

> The war is not against your spouse; it is against the things that come to steal, kill and destroy.

before you stand before God and witnesses to say, "I DO."

If you are married and didn't know or think to consider any of the above before you exuberantly made your vows, and if abuse is not an issue, it is not too late to divorce-proof your relationship. To do so, divorce should never be an option; do not put it on the table as a possibility neither before you marry nor after you marry. Recognize that the war is not against your spouse. Remember, it is the two of you together who are fighting against those things that come to kill, steal, and destroy your becoming and remaining one united front.

Let's Do It!

Consistent actions are needed to divorce-proof your marriage. These actions include keeping foolish people and their voices out of your affairs. You should never share your moments of conflict with or vent to those who have no wisdom to impart or are ill-equipped to speak life and love into your relationship. Remember, there is power in the tongue, and you will have what you say—negative or positive. Cease from comparing your relationship to someone else's. What you see may look green, but the soil beneath may not be healthy. Keep dating your spouse. Go out! Catch a movie. Go to dinner. Take a walk and hold hands. Schedule time just for the two of you. When there is discord, repent and forgive quickly. Get help when you need it; don't hesitate. Connect with a mediator—a relationship coach, counselor, or both.

10

Be Expressive

"There is a language in the eyes, the cheeks,
the lips; even the legs and feet speak ."

William Shakespeare (adapted)

*I*n marriage, self-expression is necessary. It is one of the best forms of authenticity. It is through mutually healthy expression that a couple grows and develops into their best selves. Just as it is important to express affection, it is equally important to express difference of opinion.

Yet, it doesn't always come easy to bare your soul when feelings are involved. To do so creates a sense of vulnerability, and so often we run away from exposing ourselves—even to the love of our lives—for fear of being harmed (e.g. Will what

> *Vulnerability is not weakness.*

I say be viewed as weakness and used against me?) For the record, vulnerability is not weakness; it is to be transparent from a position of strength—choosing to be present and open in this moment. As a matter of fact, studies have revealed that holding our peace when we shouldn't and internalizing negative feelings—leaving them unspoken—is harmful to both our physical and emotional well-being. So, instead of making the relationship stronger, silence at the wrong time and for the wrong reasons can weaken the relationship. How do we know this? We know this because of the experience of life, which is like the art of drawing but without an eraser.

When we look back at our journey, we see the scars--though healed--that our inability to express ourselves caused. The question, "What's wrong?" The answer, "Nothing." We were actually being dishonest by asking a question we didn't really want answered and lying because we didn't want our words to ignite into anger. We say one thing with our mouths when our body language is saying something completely different. The mouth says,

> Turn the volume of negative energy way down.

"Nothing is wrong," while the body says, "I really

hate you right now!" If not dealt with, this becomes a cycle that will have you in the wilderness traveling around a mountain and going nowhere.

It is for this reason that we must say what we mean and mean what we say, but slamming doors and cabinets is not a good way to get your message across. It is important to turn the negative-energy volume way down in order to express yourself without debilitating your spouse.

Let's Do It!

Speak up; be honest about how you feel while remaining aware and not neglecting consideration of your spouse's emotions. Don't lie. Be clear about how you feel; relaying your message in the way you want to be understood is your responsibility. Emotions can be complicated, so be careful not to over-generalize what you feel; strive for accuracy. Allow the energy of anger to cool off; when you are calm, direct your energy into words to be delivered with love and grace.

11

Be Flexible

"Man is the head of the family; woman is the neck that turns the head."

Chinese Proverb

𝓘t's unfortunate, but true, that there are a number of marriages in trouble today because the

> *In life, we go through a series of changes—desired and undesired.*

parties involved have yet to learn what it means to be flexible. The reality is that, in life, we go through a series of changes—desired and undesired—e.g. spiritual, physical, emotional, and intellectual. These changes require us to be flexible with our points of view. Unyielding personalities and the unwillingness to come to an agreement when things don't go the way one of us expects is a form of selfishness that, in and of itself, is inflexibility. Inability to negotiate and compromise in a relationship, especially when it concerns issues that are mutually beneficial, creates a stalemate, which wreaks havoc between husbands and wives.

> *Holding ground is only good when we stand together as a united front and not in opposition of each other.*

When we make the choice to hold our personal ground, it often takes place because of a history of hurt, disappointment, and/or not knowing how to do better. Despite our reasons why, holding ground is only good if, as husband and wife, we are standing together as a united front and not in opposition to each other.

Because marriage requires two people to find a happy medium, it is important for both husband and wife to be flexible and have the ability to adapt and shift between personal wants and needs and the needs of his/her spouse. This level of flexibility requires making a conscious decision and developing the skill of adaptability. Flexibility requires practice and intentionality. Being flexible to the point of loving each other through every age and stage of life creates a safe place where two

> *Learn to be flexible and bend without breaking.*

people can live and perpetually grow together as one.

Let's Do It!

Learn to be flexible and bend without breaking. You do this by adopting the *be* attitudes outlined in this book. Practice each skill by detaching and letting go of any baggage of predisposed ideas and viewpoints you may be carrying with you. Be open to new concepts and ways of thinking that will improve your aptitude for things such as problem solving and methods of effective communication. Be welcoming and supportive of the changes your spouse may go through, because changes will take place for the both of you. Be receptive to them by being aware that change is inevitable. Roll with them by flexing your muscles of love, forgiveness, and other *be* attitudes. Grow together. Embrace every age and stage of life with each other. By doing this, you can eliminate or repair any breach attempting to shatter the joy and peace that exists within your union.

12

Be Forgiving

"Forgiveness is unlocking the door to set someone free and realizing you were the prisoner."

-Unknown

ow often have we heard that forgiveness is more for the forgiver than the forgiven? Quite often, right? Yet, in our hearts, when faced with a

> It's easier said than done.

tough situation that requires forgiveness, we lean toward the motto, "Easier said than done." Why? Because when we have been wronged, hurt, and feel betrayed, a repertory of coping mechanisms kick in, and a wall of defense is erected. This mindset and associated behaviors—if not handled properly—have the potential to morph into bitterness and resentment. The challenge is finding a way to honor the truth of how we feel, and at the same time, aspire to the higher call of forgiveness. Forgiveness is the process of letting go. When we walk in the spirit of forgiveness, our anger and hurt transform into healing and peace.

> *Find a way to honor the truth of how you feel while aspirating to the higher call of forgiveness.*

Remember, forgiveness is a process. It does not mean that we forget, but that we can remember without pain or the desire for vengeance. Although we choose to forgive and say, "I forgive you," the healing may take time. Therefore, when the pain of injury resurfaces, we must be intentional to revisit the act of letting go instead of reliving the affliction.

This act of will is a path to freedom. It can help you overcome feelings of fearfulness and unhappiness, worry and agitation, indignation and resentment. When earnest forgiveness is extended, personal and relational conflicts are lifted. Although it is necessary to acknowledge your pain, it is of greater importance to choose healing, and healing comes through the power and art of forgiveness.

> *Repent and forgive as often as warranted.*

For a marriage to be successful, it is vitally important to ensure that no barriers are constructed between husband and wife. This means walking in agreement with each other—choosing to repent and forgive as often as warranted.

Let's Do It!

Understand that forgiveness is a choice, not a feeling. First, acknowledge your pain because it's okay and necessary to do so. Next, talk with your spouse—-calmly—about how he/she made you feel. Fight against negative emotions, and let go of resentment and anger in the here and now. Stop replaying the movie in your head of your spouse's infraction. Don't allow wounds to fester. Give yourself time, but make sure you're going through the process of letting it go.

Be Giving

"Intense love does not measure, it just gives."
Mother Teresa

Oftentimes, when it comes to giving, the first thing one gives thought to is money or something of a material

> There is no greater gift than genuine love and commitment.

nature. These things are fine, but there is no greater gift than the genuine love and commitment we give to each other.

Although material gifts can, and may be one's love language, materialistic endowments, while neglecting your husband or wife's spiritual, intellectual, or cultural needs, can leave him/her disappointed and desiring more. In other words, this form of giving can be deficient if it is not accompanied with the gift of your presence. It is important that we give our spouses the best and freshest of ourselves.

> *The gift that illuminates all other aspects of giving is the gift of yourself.*

We are not saying giving material gifts is of no importance. What we are saying is material gifts without the gift of yourself is not guaranteed to be fulfilling. For instance, if a relationship is abusive, an "I'm sorry" gift of jewelry or a nice vacation neither takes away nor excuses the abuse.

The gift that illuminates all other aspects of giving is the gift of yourself. Giving of self is simply sharing quality time and laughter, encouragement and respect. It is as simple and complex as being generous with your presence without omitting other means of endowment. We like to call this holistic giving.

Foster a connection with your spouse that is beyond description.

We believe that holistic giving is the sharing of life and mind, space and time. It is the ultimate form of giving that makes those you love feel and know they are important. When you give at this level, your spouse can release and relax, knowing they're in a safe place. This level of self and unselfish giving allows you to foster a connection with your spouse that is really beyond description.

Let's Do It!

Set a goal to perpetually spend quality time with your spouse daily. Give your ear and your undivided attention to your spouse everyday. Give LOVE freely and without condition. We understand that life can be busy; however, we want to challenge you to schedule time just for the two of you to enjoy the gift of laughter by playing a game and having fun together. Take time to give the gift of encouragement by looking for opportunities to compliment your spouse and build him/her up. Give your spouse the gift of respect by showing courtesy in both

words and deeds. Always be vigilant in looking
for ways to give to each other.

14

Be Grateful

"Gratitude unlocks the fullness of life.
It turns what we have into enough, and more. It turns
denial into acceptance, chaos to order, confusion to clarity.
It can turn a meal into a feast, a house into a home, a
stranger into a friend."

Melody Beattie

One thing Mildred and I have discovered on our

What we have is greater than what comes against us.

journey to oneness is that though we are periodically faced with challenges, these challenges do not have to become our major focus. What we have is greater than anything that comes against us, and we have learned and decided to walk in the spirit of gratefulness—not only for the seemingly monumental things that happen in our lives, but also the day to day, moment by moment occurrences during our together time.

"What occurrences?" you may ask. Well, let's see. Our gratefulness includes the weathering of financial challenges due to the loss of life savings—on more than one occasion—and the loss of our first home after a terrible ice storm. These seemingly astronomical events taught us to be grateful in the moment––to be grateful for our right now. Those unexpected

> *Be grateful in the moment—for the right now.*

and unfortunate events taught us to be grateful for the love of family and friends, for the moments of sitting in front of our fireplace relaxing with each other on the sofa, for the times we share a home cooked dinner and a warm smile and for the simple acts of service, such as sharing household chores.

We are thankful for the endless benefits we are experiencing as a result of practicing gratitude, which includes more positive emotions, feeling more alive, the ability to be more compassionate and kind, and the added and favorable benefit of experiencing better health.

We've learned to be grateful and thankful in the moment for the things we are blessed to secure and sustain. We've learned to appreciate and

Life is precious.

cherish the fall outs and the fall ins—the disconnects and reconnects—because life is precious and acknowledgement and awareness of this is a reward within itself.

Let's Do It!

Identify the great in your relationship and be grateful. It is the great that you saw, felt, and believed in when you uttered the two words, "I DO." It may be dormant, but it has not disappeared. Revive it!! Sit in a quiet place, close your eyes, think of all the positive reasons you chose to love the one you married, open your eyes, and write them down. Now, say, "Thank you!" As we were taught as children, those two words go a long way. Write your spouse a letter expressing what you are grateful for concerning him/her. Decide to walk in gratefulness from this day forward.

15

Be Happy

"Happiness cannot be traveled to, owned, earned, worn, or consumed. Happiness is the spiritual experience of living every minute with love, grace, and gratitude."

Denis Waitley

What if we told you that your spouse is not responsible for your happiness? We imagine

> A jaw-dropping truth.

many jaws dropped hearing this, but let's explore this concept.

What is happiness? Happiness is defined as being delighted, pleased, or glad over a particular thing. This definition, however, leans to one's happiness being rooted in happenstance, the chance occurrence of either negative or positive things happening in one's life. If we agree with this meaning, it indicates that we believe the only way we can be happy is to be perpetually enchanted, charmed, and amused on this journey through life. It would mean that without positive extrinsic stimulation, our fate would be that of doom and gloom, sorrow and dejection, heartbreak and despair.

> *Unrealistic expectations inhibit our happiness.*

Unfortunately, and in like manner. in many marriages, our happiness is commonly embedded in our deep-seated, and often unrealistic expectations surrounding what our partner should and should not do to make us happy. If our expectations are unmet, then we blame our spouses for not ensuring that we remain in good spirits. In light of this, cheerfulness can be as fickle and inconsistent as the changing wind, when we allow our state of happiness to be related directly to what happens to us.

Let's go deeper. Is it fair to project the responsibility of our happiness upon others, including our spouses? The answer is simply, no. Real and lasting joy is intrinsic. The truth is, each of us must take

Our desire is that God... will infuse our lives with an abundance of joy and peace.

responsibility for our own happiness. Although Marc and I are happy with each other and contribute to each other's happiness by sharing laughter, or a smile as we catch each other's eye across a crowded room, we learned that in order for us to be deeply and firmly grounded in happiness, it had to be rooted in each of our personal relationship with God and also how we view and relate to our personal selves.

It is in God that we can be glad and rejoice and where we can find pleasure and delight. Our desire is that God, the source of all hope, will infuse our lives with an abundance of joy and peace. By understanding where our happiness comes from, we can genuinely share our inner joy with each other. Because each of us is now walking in this truth, we've found that our intrinsic happiness collides with each other, and this happiness can be and often is infectious.

Let's Do It!

Develop a life of happiness by first building a close relationship with the Eternal One. This can be done through prayer, meditation, and reading the Word. Then begin practicing optimism—look on the bright side of things. Understand that what you think and feed your mind matters. Believe that you are fearfully and wonderfully made. It is up to you to shift your thinking by speaking the Word over and into your own life. "Fill your mind with beauty and truth. Meditate on whatever is honorable, whatever is right, whatever is pure, whatever is lovely, whatever is good, whatever is virtuous and praiseworthy" (Philippians 4:8). Savor the positive experiences and moments in your life and marriage. Look in the mirror and smile. Tell yourself, "I have joy unspeakable! I am happy!" It may feel phony in the beginning, but the more you speak and practice being happy when you see yourself, a greater extent of joy will rest within and upon you, exhibiting fullness of life and exuberance.

16

Be a Hearer

"Listening is a commitment and a compliment."
Matthew McKay

The truest form of communication is listening to the point of actually hearing (acknowledging, regarding, and understanding) the heart of the person who is

> Hear the heart of your spouse and others.

sharing his/her thoughts and/or feelings. In marriage, hearing one another is vital to the health and longevity of your relationship.

I must confess that there was a time in our marriage that Marc's and my communication would go through wild and unpredictable changes. Although we thought we were doing a decent job at listening to each other, we would often clash when what he said didn't match what I heard, and what he heard didn't match what I said. Before we fine-tuned our communication skills, it was difficult for us to really hear each other. We went through every communication block there was including filtering, mind reading, daydreaming, and capitulating. We heard what we wanted to hear and filtered out the rest. We disregarded and cast suspicion

> *We thought we were doing a decent job.*

upon each other and interjected our own ideas of what one thought the other was going to say—-before they even said it. From time to time, we would just tune each other out and allow our minds to wonder. For me, rather than engaging in a sparring match, placating was an easy out. These vices obstructed our attention and our abilities to hear accurately. The "he said, she heard, she said, he heard" way of communicating was like being on an extended rollercoaster ride.

Our greatest challenge in communication resulted from our inadequate skills and ability when conversing about situations surrounding our families of origin. Because of the different ways we were domesticated as we grew up--him from a nuclear family and me from a single-parent household—our philosophies of

> Seek the heart of God.

living and being did not always mesh. For a long time, I felt uncovered and unprotected by him when it came to his family dynamics, and getting him to see that proved to be a test of my ability to express myself with clarity. However, since we both confessed that we were King's kids, I decided that what I seemed unable to get across to him, God could. Because my husband was and is a man who would also seek the heart of God, I believed that the spirit in him would receive from the Spirit of our Father. With this in mind, I prayed, and I waited to be led by the Spirit for the right timing to express myself again. When I stopped trying to fix it, our Creator King opened both our ears and hearts, so we could hear with precision.

I will never forget the moment Marc and I had a discussion concerning something that happened within our extended family relationship concerning our daughter. It proved to be a challenge to get him to really hear me with the evidence of understanding my point about what had transpired. I remember the early

> *There is a sense of freedom that comes with being heard by the one you love.*

morning conversation as I was getting dressed. This thing that I had been trying to get across finally resonated not only in his ears, but it touched his soul, and to hear him say, "I hear you," with sincere unadulterated understanding gave me life. It felt like a weight had been lifted off my shoulders, and I experienced a sense of freedom that I could really express myself honestly and freely to the man I love. This was a real turning point in our ability to communicate effectively with each other.

Let's Do It!

When your spouse is expressing him or herself, pay attention. Listen to hear, provide feedback, and waive any judgment. When you respond, be candid, open and honest. Put aside any distracting thoughts and look directly at your spouse. Make sure your body language is open and reveals that you are genuinely interested in what he/she has to say. Allow your spouse to finish what they have to say before asking questions and don't interrupt with counter arguments. When it is time to provide feedback, reflect on and paraphrase what you heard—e.g. "What I heard you say is..." If necessary ask questions to gain clarity--e.g. "Explain what you meant when you said..." Make sure that in your listening to hear and understand that you treat your spouse in a way he/she wants to be regarded.

17

Be Healthy

"To enjoy good health, to bring true happiness to one's family...one must first discipline and control one's own mind..."

Buddha

As we work to improve our communication, understanding, and other "Be" attitudes, it is also

> *We are spirit, soul, and body.*

important to consider the role our personal health plays in our relationships. We believe that part of having a strong, healthy marriage is to have a strong, healthy self.

Because we are triune beings—as highlighted in Genesis 2:7--body (flesh), spirit (intangible consciousness), and soul (intellectual and emotional consciousness), we should be mindful of each aspect of the self as it relates to health. Health is more than the mere absence of disease and infirmity. It is a state of well-being and well-roundedness within the three points of ourselves that make us who we are. This provides the means for us to lead a full life. When we take care of ourselves physically, our bodies have the capacity to work at peak performance. A

> *We must be intentional creatures and not neglect taking care of every part of us.*

healthy soul builds our capacity to enjoy life, to bounce back, to get our bearings when life happens, to be successful, and to feel safe and secure. Nurturing the spirit through meditation, positive thoughts and words, and doing life with meaning and purpose is also a core component of our overall wellness. Because the spirit, soul, and body equals one whole of who we are, we must be intentional creatures and not neglect taking care of every part of us. To be lax about one part is to cause another part to be impaired, which we believe is not the desire of any living being. So, let's make sure we are putting forth our best effort to enhance the sum total of who we are and bring balance to our whole man.

Why is this important to marriage? It is important because having a healthy self allows us to adequately give to our spouses. Mildred and I believe that by taking better care of ourselves, we can better care for each other.

> Nourish your mind, body, and spirit.

We realize we have a responsibility to each other to do what we can to maintain good physical, emotional, and spiritual health.

We choose to work on increasing our knowledge and engaging in healthy wholesome practices that nourish our minds, bodies and spirits. We do this by exercising, meditating, preparing, and eating healthy meals. We aspire to adhere to the old adage, "Physician heal thyself." Therefore, it is essential to put into practice things that will allow our bodies to do what they are naturally created to do, to function at their highest potential and to heal itself as it was designed. Let us be enlightened by this fact. The power that made our bodies, heals our bodies; the power that breathed the spirit of life into the body supplies balance to the wholeness of man—spirit, soul, and body. Remember, faith without

> Faith without works is dead.

works is D-E-A-D. Therefore, our faith requires that we work on each of the three dimensions of ourselves.

To neglect our responsibilities regarding any facet of ourselves creates a deficit in our ability to respond to each other's needs. Because Mildred and I desire to lead full lives, we engage in practices that promote health and wellness. We understand that maintaining a healthy mind, body, and spirit requires consistent and intentional effort so we can experience a long-lasting, healthy, sustainable, sexually-

> Work on being healthy and whole.

fulfilling marriage. We work on being healthy and whole for ourselves individually and for each other so we can experience and do life together with renewed youth, so we can finish strong, and we want the same for you.

Let's Do It!

Meditate regularly to improve your memory, attention, mood, immune system, sleep, and creativity. Exercise. Lift weights, do aerobics, and/or walk regularly. When possible, do these things together. Listen to classical music. It is good for the mind, will increase brain power, help you sleep better, and improve your mood. As often as possible, opt for natural remedies. Holistic health practitioners, herbs, the right foods, and aromatherapy create conditions that promote healing for your overall well being. See a medical doctor if needed.

18

Be Honest

"Honesty is such a lonely word.
Everyone is so untrue.
Honesty is hardly ever heard
and mostly what I need from you."

Billy Joel

Honesty in a relationship, especially marriage, is one of those ideas that should be stamped in big bold letters,

> "Honesty is more than not lying."

NON-NEGOTIABLE. "Honesty," as asserted by American religious leader, lawyer, and politician, James Faust, "is more than not lying. It is truth telling, truth speaking, truth living, and truth loving." It is being willing to tell the truth in love and being able to listen and hear truth in the same vain. When the foundation of honesty is firm, it adds value to your relationship by:

* Supporting you through challenges. You can walk in confidence knowing you can depend on each other.

* Strengthening you. In the midst of tragedy, adversity, tribulation, affliction and misfortune, it helps you to stand together.

* Fortifying your marriage. It protects against outside temptations and influences

trying to seep in and weaken your relationship.

According to the Book of books, if we love life and relish the chance to enjoy good things, we should keep our tongues from evil and our lips from speaking deceit, turn away

> "Seek peace and pursue it."

from evil and do good; seek peace and pursue it (Psalm 34:12-14). What better place to demonstrate these principles than in our marriages? Remember, in marriage, our relationships should serve as a reflection of Christ's relationship to His bride— the Church. Therefore, as a married couple, we should hate what our Father hates, and love what He loves. With this being said, we, like

> Let's work to ensure that the actions we take in marriage reflect the likeness of the Originator of our lives.

our Creator King, should hate a lying tongue and should make a conscious choice to be honest in our relationships. This means hiding or engaging in wrongdoing, using inappropriate language, and/or delighting in improper behavior should not be entertained.

As people of the Book, we all strive to be the best version of ourselves and a reflection of what is good and right in relationship to our Creator King. With this in mind, let's work to ensure that the actions we take in marriage reflect the likeness of the Originator of our lives.

Let's Do It!

Make sure your actions match your words. Honesty is not just your words; it's how you live and love. Share your feelings openly and allow your spouse to do the same without bias or judgement. Avoid holding suspicions in your mind by having honest conversations. Let your life be the living and loving truth you have for each other.

19

Be Intentional

"Intention coupled with action is of great value."
Mildred Clark

Being intentional is the premeditation of discovering how to love and appreciate your spouse

> To be intentional is putting the philosophy of the heart into practice.

the way he/she desires and deserves. It moves

beyond the imagination into deliberate direction and action. To be intentional is putting the philosophy of the heart into practice. It is a consistency of conscious patterns of thought and energy. When we are intentional, we are more discerning, which allows us to see and create a loving, caring, and peaceful environment with more precision, passion, authenticity, and clarity.

Deliberateness is a tool that can be used as a means to aid in the creation, building, and sustainability of a strong, healthy, and progressive relationship. When we are deliberate about how we treat and what we do for and to each other, we make a major impact in each other's lives.

> *Intentionality offers us the ability to build capacity in our marriages.*

Being intentional about how we treat and what we do for each other is vital. Why is it so important? It is important because at the end of a wedding ceremony, two individuals who are pronounced husband and wife begin their perpetual journey to oneness. Becoming ONE is not automatic. It is intentionality that offers us the ability to build capacity in our marriages. It is deliberately setting out to learn and develop tools that will help us improve and retain skills, knowledge, and human resources needed to competently move our marriages from good to great.

To this end, this section of our writing is to cry loudly that each of the attitudes presented in this book do not necessarily come naturally between two

> LOVE means nothing if it is demonstrated as hit-or-miss, casual, or careless.

people. Because of the difference in the makeup of the male and female, each spouse has to be deliberate in ensuring that how they love and serve is actually based on the needs and desires of his/her spouse. It is with openness and intent that we reveal to each other and learn from each other the specifics of one another's particular needs and desires.

Success in any of the *be* attitudes presented in this text requires forethought. Love doesn't mean a thing if how one's demonstration of it is hit-and-miss, casual, and/or careless. Being intentional can transform your relationship from an ephemeral state to an enduring trait— from a fleeting feeling to a lasting way of being.

Let's Do It!

Take a look at each of the preceding and succeeding *be* attitudes we have discussed. Assess which attitude you need to improve and commit to being intentional about taking action to become better. Come together with your spouse and discuss how you can be better and what you genuinely need from your relationship. Together, agree that you are willing to be intentional in doing the work. Once this time of discovery has taken place, adjust your attitude accordingly, and always be mindful of and intentional about doing so.

20

Be Intimate

"Intimacy is being seen and known as the person you truly are."

Amy Bloom

Intimacy is more than the sexual escapades that take place in the bedroom, on the floor, against the wall, or on

> *Intimacy is one of the foundational blocks of marriage.*

top of the washing machine on spin cycle. It is warmth, closeness, and trust. Intimacy is one of the foundational blocks of a strong, healthy, and sustainable marriage where security and trust is experienced. It is to know your spouse deeply, and to be deeply known by your spouse. Because intimacy requires openness and vulnerability, it is often left undiscovered though it is longed for by many.

> *Intimacy is willingly giving and receiving.*

Intimacy is willingly giving and receiving through genuine personal sharing in which each spouse allows access to his and her most personal self—things you think but don't say; things you feel but don't emote; and things you know but do not tell. Intimacy is heartfelt conversations and quality moments where both parties are free to be themselves without judgment or fear of someone trying to fix or change them. The art of intimacy—at its highest level-—is the ability and willingness of two people to safely bare their souls to each other.

When two people are in it to win it, there is great benefit from a couple's ability to reveal their innermost feelings-—e.g. phobias, apprehensions, disappointments, dreams, desires, joys, and laughter. Intimacy is to think of another person as you would think of yourself. This is a beautiful act of love.

The development of intimacy, in all of its particular parts, requires mindfulness, diligence, and intentionality. It requires you to pay attention to each other to the point that you are in touch with each other's souls—being aware of your spouse's hopes, dreams, and fears. This is where two people create a place of

> *Connection between two people is enhanced when they work to create an intimate bond in which both parties feel secure and loved.*

safety—a place where you know each other so deeply that you sense when your spouse is out of sync, and you can help bring them back to a point of balance.

Oftentimes, people assume that the romantic notion of soul-mating comes with built-in intimacy; this is a fallacy. Although it is possible to connect with someone instinctively and intuitively, there is still work required to build a long-standing and intimate connection with your spouse, and openness and vulnerability are part of the process. The reality is that the connection between two people is enhanced when they work to create an intimate bond in which both parties feel secure and loved and where trust and communication abound.

Let's Do It!

Interact with each other in ways that will help your intimacy grow. It is during your quality time that you should be able to bare your souls to each other. In the midst of the joy and laughter you share, be bold in facing and having deeply emotional conversations. Rest assured, intimacy will grow when you commit to getting to know your spouse in an intrinsic and transparent way and allowing yourself to become known in the same way by him or her. Remember, carving out quality time creates opportunities for you to engage in profound conversations. In this space in time, you should create an atmosphere where matters of the heart can be shared safely and genuinely. This is intimacy at its best.

21

Be Loving

"Being deeply loved by someone gives you strength, while loving someone deeply gives you courage."

Lao Tzu

Being Loving, which is the act of true love, is a major key to a happy and fulfilling marriage. It goes beyond selfishness and self-interests.

> **Walk the talk of LOVE.**

Being loving is walking the talk. It is when words are accompanied by actions. Our actions of love should serve to nurture and have a positive effect on our spouses' self-esteem and sense of well-being. When and if our actions fail in echoing the words we speak, then what we say represents falsehood, dishonesty, empty talk, and posturing. This is not what we want. We want our love to be genuine and expressed through our actions. We must remember that actions do indeed speak louder than words.

> *True LOVE is not a feeling.*

True love, the kind of love that keeps a couple together for a lifetime, is not a feeling. It's an attitude. It's a way of thinking about and considering your spouse and letting them know they matter. Being loving is when we choose to act beyond our feelings and commit our wills to our spouses' needs and best interests regardless of the cost. It is not only what we do when things are good but how we respond and what we do during high-energy moments—moments when a couple seem to be clashing like titans because feelings have come into play. When you are loving, you take the time to reflect on your responses.

When Mildred and I coach couples, and conversations arise about tense moments that turn into arguments, we often ask them to consider a baseball game and the roles of the pitcher and the catcher. If the catcher decided to pitch to the pitcher from his/her position while the pitcher is pitching—because they're on the same team— one or both would get hurt, right? This can be viewed

> *Being loving is to allow ourselves to fully value our spouses for who they are.*

> Active LOVE will keep you from taking it personal.

similarly in marriage. During an intense moment in a loving marriage relationship, the husband or wife need to choose to be the catcher, while the other pitches. Active love will keep you from taking your spouse's temporary indignation personal. Instead, you prepare yourself to take the impact of their unabusive truth, and thereby. be instrumental in helping them to find their balance within themselves. Keep in mind that you're on the same team, and your love will be instrumental in keeping you together.

So, to ensure that our relationships do not falter, it's important we continue to take actions that our partners perceive as loving, instead of looking to our spouses to solely meet our own needs. Being loving is to allow ourselves to fully value our spouses for who they are and recognize the joy they contribute to our lives. It is showing love in a way your spouse needs and desires to be loved—a love filled with compassion, kindness, and grace.

> LOVE is not sporadic; it is consistent.

As a man, I (Marc) have found that walking the talk of love is necessary in living out the Word, which states that a man is to love his wife as Christ loved the church and gave Himself for it. With this in mind, I endeavor to recognize and love my wife the way she desires to be loved, whether that's through the love language of affirmations, gifts, physical touch, acts of service, and/or quality time. These things are not sporadic; they are consistent efforts to connect and ensure our relationship remains strong, healthy, and sustainable.

Let's Do It!

Discover your's and your spouse's love languages by taking the Five Love Language Quiz developed by author and pastor Gary Chapman. Go to:

https://www.5lovelanguages.com/quizzes/.

Once you know your languages of love, act accordingly. Do the things that minister to your spouse in his/her particular love language. For instance, if your spouse's love language is gifts, make sure you shower them with meaningful goodies. It is not about the expense, it's about the thoughtfulness of the present. If your spouse's love language is words of affirmation, speak positively into his/her life. Use words to let him/her know you appreciate them; tell them about the best part of the day you spent with them; say, "I love you" with meaning. For acts of service, help with household chores: stay up with the baby and change diapers, cook a meal, or paint a room together. Physical touch is as simple as passing by your spouse and touching them on the arm, patting their caboose, or giving a tight hug. It can also be as provocative and sexually arousing as you desire. If quality time is important, make sure that life does not get so busy that you neglect spending time with each other. Make time for dates. Go to a movie. Go for a walk. Cuddle on the couch. Just spend time together in a way that is mutually fulfilling by intentionally doing things that speak your spouse's love language.

22

Be Prayerful

"… pray for one another… Your prayers are powerful when they are rooted in a righteous life."
James 5:16

"M ay the 'force' be with you,"—a phrase frequently used in the Star Wars' movies— comes to mind as we begin this part of our

> Pray for each other not about each other.

discussion. As Marc and I consider the "force," we have come to understand the greatest force in the life of a believer is the Spirit of the Eternal One, and we have full access to Him through the power of prayer.

Often in marriage, however, instead of praying for our spouses, we build walls of defense when faced with conflict. Instead of walking in the spirit of unity, we take the unfavorable route of dealing with contention by lashing out at, criticizing, condemning, and berating the one we vowed to love, honor, and cherish. At one point, I had to ask myself, "How is that working for you?" The answer was, it wasn't working.

> *Pray earnestly for your spouse.*

Why didn't it work? It did not work because during our periods of conflict filled with high-levels of negative energy, we struggled to communicate effectively. The struggle was real and equally exhausting. We were as the children of Israel. It was as if we were wandering in the wilderness as they did for 40 years. This analogy alone caused me to be intentional about spending quality time in prayer and meditation. This set the stage for me to refocus my attention—on my relationship with God first and then with my husband. I found that when I began to pray earnestly for my husband and our union, the atmosphere and energy shifted in a positive direction. Praying sincerely for our relationship gave God, our Creator King, the license to have heavenly influence in our lives as we forged ahead in doing life together.

> *The Power of prayer does not rest in the eloquence of our words.*

Even if my prayers were awkward and my attempt feeble, it was during my quiet moments of mindful prayer and meditation that I discovered the power did not rest in the eloquence of my words. It rested in the sincerity of my heart and the Eternal One who is listening and hears. Moreover, during my quiet time, I would discover things about how I prayed for my husband and our marriage. With this knowledge, I made a fundamental change in my approach and underlying assumptions. I discovered that oftentimes I wasn't praying for my husband; I was praying about him. For instance, instead of praying that Marc would perpetually grow into being and becoming the man God created him to be, I would pray— more accurately, complain—about my dissatisfaction, disappointment, anger and aggravation. There is nothing in the latter type of invocation that is uplifting towards my blessing—the man who chose me to be his wife. He did not need the negative energy I perpetuated. He needed me to be the woman designed for him —one who could and would walk beside him as a helpful companion, a complementary counterpart.

> *Prayer unleashes the power of God in our lives.*

One thing I knew then and now know is that my husband is a man of valor who loves God as I do. So, what better way to initiate change than to recognize and honor the fact that both he and I belong to God before we belong to each other. Beginning to sincerely walk in this knowledge was freeing. I realized that what I could not change in our relationship, Father could. I knew that the closer and more connected to God he is, the closer and more connected we would be as a unit. It is prayer that unleashes the power of God in our lives and grants us the capacity to create a climate in which we can do life together in a positive, healthy, and fruitful manner. When we give the Eternal One earthly license for heavenly influence, we experience necessary paradigm shifts. Times of devotion are important to this end. These times aid in keeping me centered and focused on what is most significant and helps Marc and me to maintain a strong, healthy relationship.

Let's Do It!

Do a self check. Reflect on how you present your spouse to the Eternal One. Are you complaining about or praying for him/her? If you find you are complaining, you must shift in order to create a joyful and peaceful atmosphere within your marriage. Even if things are not as ideal as you desire, sincere prayer and meditation will increase your spiritual awareness and empower you to change direction from the state of dissatisfaction and annoyance to a state of peace and contentment. It will give you the wherewithal to earnestly pray for the wholeness and wellbeing of your spouse in every area of his/her life. Use the prayer below to begin.

Father, I pray that you protect my husband's time at home. Help him to govern our house in wisdom and fear of You. Lead and guide him in your will and your way, that he may be an example to his family at home and to the world. Give him insight into who You are in his life. Help him to find the perfect balance of his time that nothing will be lacking or wanting at home, work, and other areas of life. Help him to understand how to love me better as his wife and help me learn to be patient, loving, and appreciative toward the blessing, the man you have given me in Your chosen vessel. Enlighten him and mold within him a heart that is gentle and kind with our family. Teach me the power of unity and submission. Let us be an example of Your love and relationship to your bride, the church. In Yehushua's (Jesus') name, Ashé (Amen).

Although this is a wife's prayer for her husband, we want husbands to understand that it is just as important for you to pray earnestly for and not about your wives.

23

Be a Safe Place

"The person you love should be where you can calm your soul. They should be your safest place to be yourself. Life is hard enough, so that person should be your solace."
Unknown

When Marc and I got married, I neither thought, nor did I know, anything about the term "safe place." However, this is exactly what I expected him to be for

> *You should not expect your spouse to be a greater place of safety than you are to him.*

me. Like many women, I expected my husband to be this strong, robust guy that would keep me safe and secure in every way. I never really considered that he, too, needed to feel safe with me as well. The truth of the matter is, we're in this thing together. We each need to know that we have each other's back, and we will do each other no harm.

I realized that I should not expect my husband to be a greater place of safety for me than I was for him. I have found that oftentimes

> *Dismantle harsh judgements and destructive criticisms.*

we women tend to assume that our men's feelings are not felt by them as intensely as our own. This could not be further from the truth. The reality is that Marc has feelings and emotions too, and I have come to understand that even though he may express his feelings differently, they are no less fervent. I personally had to STOP ignoring this truth.

I had to begin the process of being intentional about not ignoring his needs. I dismantled my engaging in harsh judgements, destructive criticisms, and any other harmful interactions. I replaced these things with deliberate attention to his body language, the timber of his voice, the look in his eyes, and the way he held his head. I found that when I am

> Ensure that you are a companion of strength and power.

intentional about fulfilling my husband's needs, and choose to know him in a very real way, I am more cognizant of when he has had a hard day or is disappointed or disheartened about something. This perception allows me to make necessary adjustments in my own thinking and/ or behavior to ensure that I am a companion of strength and power and serve as a safe place for him, and he does the same for me.

We are perpetual in our efforts to create a space where each of our need to feel safe is honored—a space where we are secure in our ability to confess when we mess up and offer an apology without being afraid of retaliation. It's important to be safe enough to remove the mask so often worn to avoid confrontation or conflict.

> *Take off your mask.*

Paul Laurence Dunbar's poem, We Wear the Mask, can be applied, because even in marriage, there may be times when spouses will engage in one or more of the following:

❖Wearing a mask that grins and lies. Hiding our cheeks and shading our eyes.

❖Smiling to keep from crying, when our hearts are torn and bleeding.

❖Being subtle when on the inside we want to scream.

❖Only showing what we want or think the other person desires or needs to see.

However, it is important for us to not wear masks harbored in fear and pride and to hide hurts and/or wrongs. We need to be free to let them out knowing that we will

> *Release your fears and anxieties that we may have unknowingly brought into the relationship.*

receive love, grace, and forgiveness when necessary. It is of great significance here that we also understand that in order for our spouses to be safe places, we must release our fears and anxieties that we may have unknowingly brought into the relationship due to other relational experiences. In other words, being a safe place is about trusting our spouse to be a source of refuge, strength, and support and also choosing to be the same for them.

LET'S DO IT

Take about five minutes to examine yourself by reflecting on two things: 1) Do I trust my spouse to be a safe place? Why or why not? If there is a lack of trust, what energy are you bringing that contributes to it? 2) Are you a safe place for your spouse? Can your spouse be fully who he/she is with you? Why or why not? Are you approachable, or are you on edge when your spouse decides to take off his/her mask and attempt to engage in difficult conversations. After you have been intentional and mindful of your endowment in creating a safe place, we pray you will make the paradigm shift to grow or enhance this **be** attitude. How?

Have a spirit of gratitude towards your spouse. Receive each other's compliments, gifts, time, attention, affection, attraction, sex, and more—graciously and joyously. Willingly extend grace, mercy, and forgiveness to each other in a healthy way. Give criticism only if it is constructive; make sure the timing is acceptable. Give your spouse your full attention when he/she is talking. Never tear each other down to others. Decide to trust your spouse to be a safe place and ensure that you are a safe place for your spouse—being free to share with and receive the fullness of the person you married.

24

Be Transformed

"Do not allow this world to mold you in its own image. Be transformed from the inside out by renewing your mind."

Romans 12:2 (VOICE)

*T*he United Negro College Fund has a slogan that has been around for decades. The slogan is, "A Mind is a Terrible Thing to Waste," and it is. It is also a powerful force.

> *Think about the positive, the good, the beauty.*

What one believes—good or bad—is what one attracts. For this reason, it is important to think and speak things that are filled with beauty and truth, things that are honorable and pure, lovely and good, virtuous and praiseworthy. This level of thinking brings with it a peacefulness that transcends our limited understanding. When it comes to our spouses, it allows us to see each other with clarity and walk the talk of love created by two people who are committed to the journey of ONE. This level of thinking requires transformation from old patterns and examples and moves us from a negative to a positive disposition.

Transformation is required in marriage because we carry with us all of who we are and bring it into the union, whether we are aware of it or not. Not only do we bring our personal way of thinking, we also bring the domesticated training each of us received within

> It is necessary to individually explore who you truly are.

our individual households, which includes understanding, beliefs, and values. Some of the things we learned may be ideas and opinions we have to be willing to change for the betterment of our marriages.

When two people decide to deviate from an established pattern of aloneness and go on an excursion of two becoming one, it is necessary for them to explore who they truly are individually. They should review their separate perspectives. Then, they must determine what each of them needs to alter in order to give 100% of themselves to each other, beyond any preconceived notions. This type of self-

> *Transformation begins on the inside.*

reflection makes a difference because it causes us to face ourselves and can help us understand that it is okay to make positive changes that transform us.

This transformation begins on the inside; it stems from what we think and believe. When considering this inside out transformation, I am reminded of a time when my thinking was tired. I, Mildred, spoke tiredness over my life for weeks. I audibly spoke the words, "I'm tired. I'm so tired," all through the day. One day, I realized I was attracting what I was speaking. This realization caused me to immediately shift my thinking, and the tiredness I felt was lifted. In the same way, I had to cease and desist in my stinking thinking as it related to my marriage. Now, instead of thinking and speaking the negative, I think on and speak the positive. I choose to live a life of transformation through self-

> *Check yourself.*

reflection. I check myself instead of checking my husband. I question my motives instead of my husband's motives. I ponder and examine my established realities to determine whether they are indeed realities or self-inflicted, unprofitable beliefs in need of a fundamental change in approach and underlying assumptions. More often than not, it is the latter, and transformation is needed. Making this adjustment led me to enjoy a more fulfilling, strong, healthy, and enduring union.

Let's Do It!

Let's do a mental self-check. Go to a quiet place. Sit comfortably. Close your eyes, and check your thoughts regarding your relationship with your spouse. Are your thoughts pure? Are they lovely? Are they praiseworthy? If not, shift your thinking. Let go of your preconceived notions of what marriage should be and look like. Understand that you will grow your marriage together. Start by renewing your mind. Think about the things that drew you to your spouse—the things that made you smile, the things that brought you joy. Make sure you let go of any preconceived notions that do not serve your marriage, and then choose to fill the atmosphere with positive vibes.

If you have difficulty pushing past the negative thoughts, ask yourself, "Is what I'm thinking true?" "Is this absolute or is it my personal reality?" "How do I react or what happens when I believe the thought is true?"

"Who would I be and how would things be different without the thought?" Are you harboring any negative thoughts about your relationship with your spouse? If so, it is an unnecessary burden that can be adjusted by turning your thoughts around. Shift your thinking, and choose a more positive path. You have the authority and the capacity to do so.

25

Be Whole

"'You are all things. DENYING, rejecting, judging, or HIDING from any aspect of your total being creates pain and results in a lack of wholeness.' [So] pay mind to your own life, your own health, and wholeness. A bleeding heart is of no help to anyone if it bleeds to death.'"

Joy Page & Frederick Buecher

*D*uring our significant and formative teenage years, we grew up under indoctrination and teaching that the major role and purpose of the woman, in marriage, was to serve the needs of her husband. There was little to no regard for the individuality of both the

husband and the wife, and no consideration of the scripture, which stated, "Submit yourselves one to the other." The distorted line of instruction regarding submission often led to a

> *Women tended to deny, reject, and hide away aspects of themselves.*

chasm between husband and wife because submission was taught as subservience from a place of inferiority and male domination. Living under the shadows of their husbands, a significant number of women tended to deny, reject, and hide away aspects of themselves, which often showed up as low self-esteem and a lack of wholeness.

In addition to the inaccurate teaching delivered within the church, we discovered that the way we lived, those who made impressions on our lives, and how we were brought up also play a contributing part to our wholeness the lack thereof. I, Mildred, am a perfect example of this. Marc and I had been married 21 years and was blessed to have three joys from heaven of our own before I realized the effect my father's absence played on my inability to be fully whole. It was during a counseling session that I experienced a lightbulb moment. During this particular session, I was questioned about my relationship with my father. Short answer, we didn't have one, and being his only blood-born child, I subconsciously felt worthless, and grappled with understanding why he chose not to be an active part of my life. Inside I was still a broken little girl, and I was angry and resentful

> *Sometimes we bring unknown and unclear expectations into our marriage.*

towards the man who was partially responsible for my existence. It wasn't until engaging in counseling that I discovered what a strong impact this had on me. Seeking help, I came to understand that a lot of my self-esteem was wrapped up in the lack of attention and love I needed and wanted from my father. Many of my emotions in my marriage were tied up in the lack of having a relationship with my him. Because I didn't get what I needed as a young girl from him, I had unknowingly placed this responsibility upon my husband.

As I began to talk about my upbringing and childhood experiences, it was uncovered, and I became cognizant that sometimes we bring unknown and unclear expectations into our marriage that we ourselves are unaware of—things that lie in the subconscious mind. These things hang over us like an acute case of the flu, but our spouses aren't even the ones

> *Displaced expectations can affect the health of your marriage.*

who made us sick. In my case, I was longing for affirmation from Marc that I never received from my father. I didn't know why it was so important, but I wanted Marc to tell me and show me in some shape, form, or fashion that I was enough. This lack of affirmation left me feeling incomplete.

Together, Marc and I set out to break these cycles. To break the cycles, we had to first come to understand the power and the strength associated with submission that was not adequately taught in

> *Seek wisdom and get understanding.*

the church. In addition to reading and meditating on the written Word, we studied and read books that offered practical guidance. We also collaborated with other wise couples and gleaned from their wisdom.

We were enlightened on our journey because we believed in the principle of gaining wisdom and understanding. We discovered that, yes, wives should submit to their husbands. We also learned that submission is not one-sided; it is important to submit to each other.

We found that the healthiest marriages are those where the husband and wife did not lose their singleness, which is, as asserted by Myles Munroe, "the state of being separate, unique, and whole." In fact, two whole people who come together can more adequately realize their united purpose as they walk jointly to fulfill the will of God in and through their union.

Coming into this knowledge also brought healing to my broken places. It allowed me to let go of what I didn't get from my earthly father, and to recognize the blessing I have in the man who chose me to be his wife. Breaking the cycle in this area required work; it required self-reflection and self-realization. I had to become reacquainted with and fully learn who I am both alone and with my spouse. I went forth and rediscovered the things that made me separate, unique, and whole.

> *What we do for and say to each other should come from a place of wholeness.*

As for Marc and me, the lesson we learned over time is that when two whole people come together in unity, compliments and affirmations are genuine and heartfelt. What we do for, and say to each other comes from our wholeness. We avoid doing or saying things simply for pacification and appeasement. We realize that wholeness breeds wholeness, and we want to continue to promote and encourage each other to be our best selves as whole individuals.

> *Walking in wholeness affords you the liberty to advance together as two complete individuals on your journey to oneness.*

Unlike the mathematically equation of $1 + 1 = 2$, when one whole man and one whole woman come together as husband and wife, they create one whole marriage ($1 + 1 = 1$). It is within this wholeness that we experience our needs being met without draining each other's energy. In other words, it's about our giving over receiving, which has resulted in each of us receiving in abundance. I feel safe in asserting that you too can experience the same.

With all of this in mind, it is our goal to help couples understand that maintaining your individuality does not prevent you from forging a new bond of wholeness in your marriage. Walking in wholeness affords you the liberty to walk together as two complete individuals in your journey to oneness.

Let's Do It!

In order to be separate, unique, and whole, you must identify and become aware of who you are independent of your spouse. Get in touch with you. Get to know the core of who you are. Identify your needs, interests, and wants. Know you are a whole person and not a fraction to be completed. This is critical to becoming and being a healthy individual and necessary in order to view yourself as a complete person with a full, happy life in front of you. Develop your sense of self. Pursue personal interests. Be yourself, and be comfortable with giving your spouse space to be themselves as well. Speak your truth without creating conflict and offense. Speak with love, care, and affection about what you need to do to be your best overall self—as an individual and in unity with your spouse. With this being said, find time to close your eyes and connect with yourself to make these discoveries.

In Conclusion

*T*he power of being is the expressed interest of this book. It is easy to talk about how we live and move, but the challenge is in being—being your best loving self in all of your relationships, especially in your marriage.

Our desire is that the sanctity of marriage remains a commitment between partners to do the perpetual work necessary to create, build, and sustain a strong, healthy union. The preceding **be** attitudes are tools you can use to walk the talk of love. It is a means to assist you in putting love in motion.

Because of our desire to make a positive impact in the lives of those we are graced to serve, prayer was rendered over each word and paragraph contained in this book. Our desire is that this reservoir of information and shared glimpses into our lives will serve you well. From our heart to yours, we want you to know you are not alone in being and becoming your best self in relationship matters, especially in marriage. The wisdom, knowledge, and enlightenment we have poured into these pages is for you—each of you who needs a sharpened countenance ignited within to do the work necessary to create, build, and sustain a strong, healthy relationship.

This resource is for those thinking about marriage, those desiring marriage, those preparing for marriage, and those who are married and seeking to thrive together as one with your spouse.

Refer to this text often as you go forth and develop the *be* attitudes that have the potential to speak and spark life first into you as an individual, and then to you and your spouse as you COMMIT TO DO THE WORK.

Notes

Notes

Notes

Notes

Notes

Notes

Made in the USA
Coppell, TX
17 June 2020